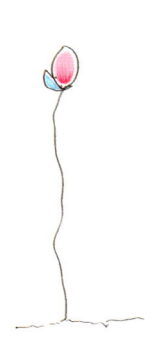

Meditation Journey of Bikkhu Jeong Yeo

A Meditation Journey for Seeking Myself

Puremind Books

Please read this book.

As you read it, your mind would feel at ease.

You can also be

A great master of meditation.

On Meditation Journey
with
Bikkhu Jeong Yeo

Just stop for a moment.

Take a moment and listen to yourself.

Feel the waves of energy within your mind.

And feel your mind as the blue sky.

Meditation makes your mind happy.

Meditation is done with mind, not with head, it is said.

Life is constantly creating thoughts and you live on despite being tired of the thoughts that you create.

Meditation and healing become invaluable when both your body and mind are suffering.

In a complicated modern society, meditation is like a life-companion.

Meditation calms life and quietens wavering mind.

A disturbed mind makes life tired, difficult, and wavering that cause distress and suffering to self.

Desire and greed, such as wealth, fame etc. may seem to make life happy, but in the end, they continue to make life stressful, difficult, and tired.

Meditation is not happiness by filling, but by emptying.

Understanding with head and concentrating on theories is not even half of meditation.

Meditation is a journey along with body, mind, and heart.

Body and mind become calm and happy on becoming one through training.

Meditation aims at understanding the root cause of fatigue and difficulties in life and its logical removal. It would be similar to a doctor's job of knowing the cause of patient's illness and treating accordingly.

There is a big difference in practicing it after understanding a little of what the self is than without knowing.

Understanding self and practicing meditation resembles clear water:

The clear water poured into a cup remains the same even on shaking.

When shaken hard, the water will move vigorously, but it will always remain the same as before.

Fully aware of self-mind, a person practicing meditation remains as pure as clear water, unstained by dirt. That is why he remains always happy.

On the other hand, practicing without understanding of self, resembles muddy water. One may feel that the mind is becoming clearer by practice and may even feel good about it, but when rattled by someone, anger and irritation burst out.

When you arrive at deep meditation through the body, mind and enlightenment, your pain, agony also disappear and the spiritual world becomes beautiful and comfortable, like the fragrance of flowers on a spring day.

This practice is about becoming confident and comfortable more and more.

Spiritual training makes soul clear and clean.

Meditation leads one to hope.

The power to freely control the mind would raise life to a higher level of happiness.

Make the mind fragrant, make the world fragrant
Bikkhu Jeong Yeo
Yeoyeojeongsa Temple, Geumosan Mountain

Fragrant Leader

Bikkhu Jeong Yeo is an invaluable person in our society, who has realized that the fundamental spirit of religion transcends religious colors and unity in diversity comes from the practice of love and compassion.

I wholeheartedly congratulate the publication of the writings of Master Jeong Yeo, whom I have always respected.

This book is definitely noble and beautiful, since writing is the expression of one's thought and reveals character of the person.

Let us all read the book of Master Jeong Yeo and try to be people with fragrant hearts. Let us be the precious ones who make everyone happy.

Father Kim Gye-chun
Fouder President
Association of Religious Leaders for Jont Action, Busan

A Great Religious Leader

Last year, I traveled to India and studied meditation. People from all over the world come to India for meditation. However, the answer is already within the self. One may not know the way though.

Meditation is the wisdom of finding the way inside one's own heart. Meditation is widely used in religion, psychology, welfare, medicine, art therapy, etc. Steve Jobs also reigned over his mind through meditation.

This collection on meditation published by Master Jeong Yeo who has practiced meditation himself for many years, remaining faithful to the basics of meditation, while explaining it in a way that anyone can understand easily. Furthermore, I am sincerely grateful for his illustrations in the book, as he is a also master of Seonhwa (meditational art) that brighten mind, deepen meditation and heal just by looking at them.

I now think of him as my older brother and follow him because of the relationship that started when he was the chief monk of Beomeosa Temple and ever since I rejoice this acquaintance.

Many people will regain their peace of mind and feel comfortable and happy while reading his meditation book. I am so happy when I think of it.

I am happy to walk hand in hand with this great monk for peace on the Korean Peninsula and for healing the world, transcending religion.

Love and peace to everyone! Om Shanti!

Pastor Bang Young-sik
International Peace Healing Center

Meditation Journey of Bikkhu Jeong Yeo
A Meditation Journey for Seeking Myself

The need for Meditation	Indeed • 27
	Musk deer • 28
	Meditation is⋯ • 31
	Why practice meditation? • 32
	Blue sky and white clouds • 34
	Tathata • 36
	Meditational healing • 38
	Mindless mind • 40
	Where does suffering come from? • 42
	Finding true self • 45
	Way to resolve conflict and fear • 46
	Cultivating the garden of mind • 48
	Mind that doesn't move ⋯ • 50
	Attachment • 52
	Meditation⋯ • 54
	Relaxed mind • 57
	Meditation • 59

Meditation Journey of Bikkhu Jeong Yeo
A Meditation Journey for Seeking Myself

Meditation · 60
Who am I? · 61
Emptying mind · 63
Make room for others · 64
Happiness of non-possession · 66
Therapy for mind · 73

Story of Seon Master Tansan · 75

Meditation Journey of Bikkhu Jeong Yeo

A Meditation Journey for Seeking Myself

The Basics of Meditation	Forms of meditation · 80
	Right posture · 83
	Cross-legged sitting meditation - lotus posture · 84
	Half-lotus posture · 86
	Like pyramid · 88
	Breathing meditation · 90
	Method of breathing meditation · 92
	Importance of breathing · 94
	Observe breathing · 96
	Just breathe with full attention · 98
	Importance of the waist · 100
	Placing of hands? · 103
	Open or close eyes? · 105
	Shape of mouth and tongue inside? · 106
	Place of meditation · 110
	Way to practice · 111

Master Hyega · 112

Meditation Journey of Bikkhu Jeong Yeo
A Meditation Journey for Seeking Myself

Kinds of Meditation
- Unobstructed mind · 116
- Illusion greated by mind · 118
- Mind without focus · 120
- Globalization of meditation · 122
- If the first learning goes stray · 124
- Walking meditation · 126
- Lying meditation · 128
- Importance of body relaxation · 131
- When distractions arise · 132
- Meditation with music · 134
- Tea-drinking meditation · 136
- Just observation is meditation · 138
- Regular meditation · 141
- While meditating · 143
- Effects of meditation · 145
- Original mind · 146

Meditation Journey of Bikkhu Jeong Yeo
A Meditation Journey for Seeking Myself

Daily Practice of Meditation

Master Seungchan · 152
Have a cup of tea! · 154
Where is the path? · 157
The base of original mind · 158
Mind that resembles home · 162
Self-satisfaction · 165
Consistent meditation · 166
If you fix it, you will be happy··· · 168
A mind like the sky · 171
Everything is one · 172
Poor habits · 174
Meditation and Karma · 177
Avoid anger · 179
When angry · 181
Meditation in everyday life · 182
Donkey's grave · 184

Meditation Journey of Bikkhu Jeong Yeo
A Meditation Journey for Seeking Myself

The
Strength of
Meditation

Why am I here now? · 196
Meditation and Samadhi · 198
A soft mind · 202
Power of concentration · 204
Calming excited mind · 207
Like pebbles · 208
Source of thoughts · 211
Transform your Karma · 213
Shadow created by thoughts · 214
I am a happy man · 217
Just watch and listen · 218
A free man · 220

The need for Meditation

True happiness cannot be found somewhere else. Paradise is in the center of your own quiet mind, is true realization.

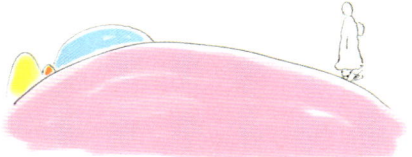

Indeed

Who am I?

Really, who am I?

Musk deer

At a particular age, musk deer emits a unique scent that emanates from its own naval scent-pocket. Intoxicated by the fragrance, the musk deer keep searching it in all directions and wonder where the fragrance is coming from! It jumps around frantically looking for the source of the scent and even falls to death from steep cliffs. It is said that countless numbers of deer suffer disaster which may seem quite absurd.

The musk deer's scent does not come from outside, but from its own belly button.

On finding out that it is coming from its own belly button, the search for it outside seizes.

While practicing meditation, the outward mind, and the mind pulled by desires, greed gradually returns to its tranquil home. True happiness does not lie elsewhere, and one realizes that paradise exists in calmness of mind. Practicing meditation allows you to know thyself and make you aware that happiness lies wherever you stay, or journey.

Meditation is⋯

Meditation is⋯

In short,

Easing thoughts

Relaxing

Calming self

Without being guided by boisterous boundaries

Outside, or inside

Making mind tranquil

Unwavering

And just comfortable.

Why practice meditation?

Probably there are times in life, not just once, or twice, when one faces various pains and sufferings. Due to business failure, financial loss, or for similar reasons while doing business for the sake of family, sustaining livelihood may not be possible, thus suffering and pain in the heart would be immense. A person would seriously contemplate how to get out of the mess when facing backlash in life, and suffering bone-chilling pain from disappointment and frustration. That person will endeavor hard in life to earn money to pay off debts and provide for his family. It is fortunate if everything turns out the way one wished, but if things do not work out well, he would terminate own life. We often see people around us vulnerable to suicide. Stop for a moment, and look back on your path trodden with a quiet mind. You must take a re-look at yourself, going back one or two steps.

Blue sky and white clouds

The primitive tribes live happily, taking care of the family dancing and singing, while living naked in jungle's natural surrounding.

Our lives begin with nature and finally return back to it. Try breathing slowly. Raise your head towards the blue sky and see. Even though the white clouds continue floating, the sky always remains blue.

Our hearts also resemble the blue sky. Wealth and fame, hate and kindness, are like floating clouds.

Empty your mind. Empty it fully like the blue sky. You must live your life with emptied mind, and without any greed, like the sky. Our original heart is pure and spotless, like that of a child.

Meditation guides us back to our pure original mind.

It leads us to escape from pain and suffering. Please let go of the painful and suffering mind. Emptying mind is more precious than filling it.

Smile brightly with a clean mind. The place where one stays has all happiness and joy.

Tathata

When meditation gets deep

And reach the peak of silence

Comes the state of samadhi when 'self' disappears

Subjectivity and objectivity fully emptied

Neither I, nor any one else exists

Existence of bright Tathata only

Leads to awakening.

Note: The term Tathata is often thought to mean either "one who has thus gone" (tathā-gata), "one who has thus come" (tathā-āgata), or sometimes "one who has thus not gone" (tathā-agata). This is interpreted as signifying that the Tathāgata is beyond all coming and going - beyond all transitory phenomena.

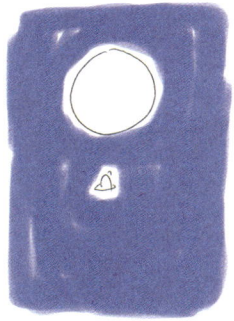

Meditational healing

Meditational healing is

Returning desultory scattered thoughts

In the tranquil mind

To the original state of mind.

It has the effect of returning

To the inherently healthy body

From the physically unhealthy body.

Meditation and healing is also a practice

That changes

Abnormalities and imbalances in body and mind

To the normal.

Changing the problem, to the non-problem state

Is called healing.

Mindless mind

This two-character word literally mean 'nothingness' and 'mind'. It means absence of mind, when explained literally.

'If you don't have a mind, wouldn't you be a dead corpse?' one may retort.

No-mind does not mean that there is no mind, but it means that the mind moves along the boundary without any attachment. It refers to a boundary that is clear, distinct and delicate.

Where does suffering come from?

There will always be suffering and joy in life, no matter where you exist. Most people think that suffering comes from outside. You may think so, but in fact, suffering originates in mind.

We need to know where the cause of suffering lies? On viewing flowing water, we know how it becomes a stream, and if we trace back the stream, we will know that water starts flowing from the valley. Just as we come to know how it flows, there must be a source for sure for all that happens.

When we consistently investigate the cause of suffering, we find that it is ignorantly in the shadow of thoughts on the surface of our mind. The shadow aspires to own buildings, cars, apartments and all kinds of jewelry. Furthermore, it creates highs and lows of fame and desire

and causes self-suffering on being lead by them.

Therefore, in order not to suffer, it is important to know that material things, fame, and desires are not something that exists in reality, but rather a shadow of thoughts drawn on the mind. It is really important to know that those things are surely not true.

The Enlightened Buddha, living in the bright light of mind, knew the shadows and illusions of suffering, and was never deceived or attracted to any of them.

Indifferent, delicate, permanent space, without any sense of attachment or abandonment is the seat of Buddha. If you know clearly that pain and anxiety are just shadows drawn by the mind, no matter wherever you are, your mind will be calm, clear, and clean.

Finding true self

In order to find true self

Thoughts that fly aimlessly around

Need to be calmed down

By resting them a bit.

This practice is true meditation

And it is the right way to train mind.

Way to resolve conflict and fear

Hostility towards others disappears by practice of meditation. Conflict arising in mind constantly is also resolved during meditation.

Both fear and conflict disappear during meditation. Medical science in USA and Europe found evidence to support that with regular practice of meditation, psychological panic disorder could be treated and restore mental health and improvement, better than medicine.

Negative thoughts will turn into positive ones if you meditate consistently. Negative thoughts darken the mind. Your life will change to happiness, if you change your thought to a positive one.

Cultivating the garden of mind

If you don't cultivate the garden of your mind,

it would resemble an uncultivated paddy field.

Grain cannot grow in the field when weeds grow thick.

Develop the power to observe your inner self.

Go back to the basics of gardening.

When you pull out the weeds of agony and delusion from the field of your mind,

it is meditation, also called practicing Seon, or Zen.

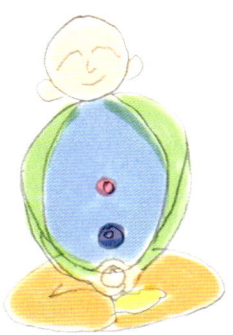

Mind that doesn't move in the face of controversy

To saints who have realized their mind

no karma can attract them.

When the mind becomes calm and clear,

one is detached from desires and greed.

Mind is neither guided by boundaries,

nor is moved by debate on right or wrong,

because it transcends everything.

A heart that does not move in the face of controversy is the mind of a saint.

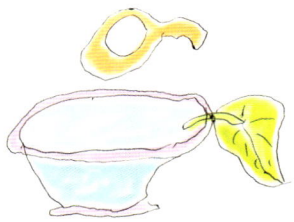

Attachment

Pain and suffering

starts with attachment.

If you look closely,

being led by the attachment to karma

is nothing but

the shadow of the mind created by thoughts,

and nothing more than an illusion,

and thus, not the truth.

The shadow is not the truth.

On realizing that it is vain,

you reach the level of sainthood

by clearly knowing your mind,

as you will not be deceived by any shape or word.

The practitioner's mind,

not guided by any boundaries,

can stay in a quiet state, where controversy disappears.

The meditative absorption (jhana) is clear and calm.

It is a pure space without any stains.

Meditation···

Meditation leads

so that one could return to true mind.

The action that takes one back to the original state

is called meditation, or healing.

Relaxed mind

If you knew your original mind,

your mind is always relaxed.

As it is not deceived

in the shadow of desire

in the shadow of greed

it is ever relaxed

wherever it stays, or travel to.

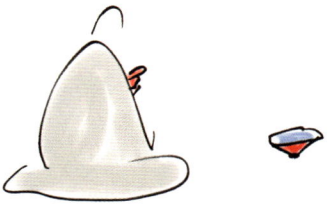

Meditation

Meditation frees you from ignorance.

It lets you find out for yourself that

greed and anger arise constantly

and teaches you the way to control craving.

Greed and anger get in the way of happiness.

Hatred, resentment, envy, and jealousy interfere with your happiness.

Laziness, anxiety, and nervousness also hinder happiness.

Meditation eliminates these wrong thoughts.

It has the power to transform you into happiness.

Meditation

If you continue to meditate,

your mind becomes relaxed and increasingly calm.

Who am I?

Busy from morning to evening

I think and think again.

Is the thought me?

Is it me who gets angry and grumpy?

Is it me who is smiling?

Is it me who is crying?

Then who am I?

Emptying mind

Try emptying your mind.
Try emptying it a little bit.

Even when you empty your mind just a little bit
life becomes happier.
An impatient and panting mind
makes life unhappy.
Just endeavoring to fill up mind,
and endless desire to possess,
makes you break away
from restoring mind to its original place.

Make room for others

Make room for others just a little bit.

If you yield just a little bit

there will be no more fighting.

Yielding a little bit,

being considerate,

is not a very difficult task.

Generously change your harsh mind

that yielded not even an inch.

Making improvements little by little is

practice of meditation.

Happiness of non-possession

You can eliminate all kinds of pain that occur in life, if you know the causes clearly. The doctor can treat a patient's illness by identifying it only by finding out the pathogen that caused the illness.

Each person feels pain differently. It is necessary to know the exact cause and depth of pain to provide appropriate treatment. It is very important to know the cause of suffering and suggest appropriate treatment.

Great saints say that the cause of suffering is endless obsession with attachment and possessiveness. Life becomes pain and suffering when constant obsession to possess and own things do not work out the way one wished.

Most people are having a hard time living their lives due to preoccupation with material things. People despair and suffer as they compare their lives with others. Many decide to end their precious life when things do not happen according to their wishes.

Saints asked us to live life of non-possession with emptied-mind.

For me, the reason to admire the life of non-possession, as shown by Bikkhu Beopjeong is from his spirit of non-possession that awakens all who have obsession with possessiveness.

What is the difference between having more and having a little less?

Is it possible to do so?

The universe shares the same grace with everyone. Just as the sun illuminates the whole world, and rain evenly soaks the world, non-possession is not something of self-possession; it means not to own anything mentally or materially.

Is it possible to live life without owning something? Birds live flying in the sky without possessing anything and fish live in water without owning anything.

Their life is free. Sky, land, sea, stars twinkling in the sky, flowing water, night sky, and the moon floating in the night do not belong to anyone special.

Everyone sees, feels, and loves them collectively. No one can own the nature as his own.

Life is becoming difficult and painful because of the obsession to own things.

It is because of the desire to do so. People are greedy for gathering wealth and possessing love, jealous for fame and strive to own all kinds of things. This possessiveness tires life.

A true saint possesses things without non-possession; utilizes material things

and love without owning them. When you utilize things without owning them, and live life with an emptied mind, you enjoy the comfort of freedom while living or leaving.

I think life is living like the clouds and the wind.

Therapy for mind

If you meditate consistently 20 minutes every day, your health will improve.
It becomes possible to treat various diseases
that occur in the mind.
When the excited mind calms down and becomes quiet,
you will return to your original healthy mind.
A person who has suffered from depression long, rapid improvement is apparent,
just one month after starting meditation.
Meditation calms the restless mind.
When mind is stable, life will be stable.
Meditate anytime, anywhere
without restrictions of space and location.

Story of Seon Master Tansan

Master Tansan was travelling with his companion monk.

He was crossing a stream one day and the water in the stream seemed not very deep. But halfway through, the water depth reached above the knees so he had to roll up his trousers.

Just then, a pretty village girl crossing the stream was seen standing in the middle of the stream, feeling helpless and embarrassed. She was embarrassed to roll her skirt up as her calves get exposed.

On seeing this, Tansan immediately went to the girl, carried her in his arms and took her across the stream without any hesitation. She was red with embarrassment, yet thanked the monk profusely and hurriedly walked away.

Master Tansan walked along comfortably as if nothing had happened, but in the eyes of the companion monk, Tansan looked like a snob. He was very upset. On the way he was busy thinking how unsuited Tansan was to pursue study or practice good deeds.

Thinking about this and that, he ended up coming to the temple. The companion monk thought this was the right time to confront Tansan, "How can you pursue to become a monk when you carry a young woman in your arms while crossing river."

"I helped her to cross the stream and soon forgot about it, but don't you still carry her in your mind?" Master Tansan replied.

Even though they studied together, Monk Tansan's mind

was indifferent and free from any obsession. It is the state of mindlessness, and nothing clung to him, or obstructed him on the way.

On the other hand, it seems that the companion monk was not free of obsessions and hurdles in his mind and was just stuck with that thought.

Mindless mind's boundary remains indifferent and do not get dirty or stained.

Helping someone in a difficult situation, without feeling any compulsion and leaving without any attachment is the act of non-attachment.

A life without any attachment is mindless mind. If you live with mindless mind, where ever the mind goes remains a paradise.

The Basics of Meditation

The most important thing for meditation is to have the right posture. It is like the process of setting the ground and laying the cornerstone to build a house.

Forms of meditation

There are many types of meditation. If you are able to calm your mind, no matter what situation you are in, you will not be shaken and your life will be happy and comfortable.

All methods of practice to achieve this state could be referred as meditation.

There are many types of meditation: breathing meditation, walking meditation, standing meditation, sitting meditation, contemplative meditation, dance meditation, mantra meditation, meditation with tea drinking, meditation while standing, lying down, chant, listening to music, and during work.

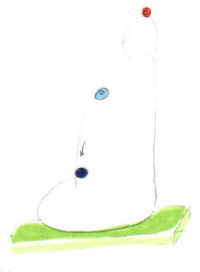

[Keep your back straight]

Right posture

The most important thing in meditation is to have right posture.

It is similar to the process of clearing the ground and laying the foundation stone when building a house.

The cornerstone must be straight and sturdy. Any house will collapse if its foundation is not right. Likewise, in practicing meditation right posture is very important.

Cross-legged sitting meditation - Lotus posture

The cross-legged sitting meditation is called lotus posture, because it is stable like a lotus flower. It is also called Tathagata-seat because it is the sitting position of Buddha. Because one feet is connected to the other, it is called a lotus posture. Cross-legged sitting may be difficult for beginners. It is placing the right ankle on top of the left thigh and then placing the left ankle on the right thigh.

The advantage of sitting cross-legged is that the back is straight and the spine is erect. The advantage lies in the fact that energy and blood flow remain smooth, while sitting long. There is not too much strain on the spine as the pelvis is straightened.

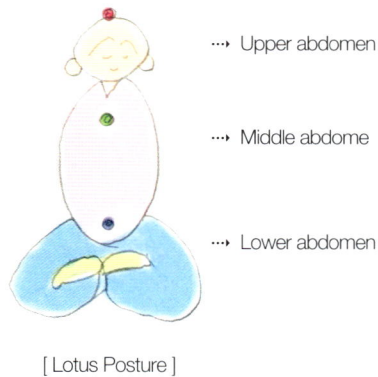

[Lotus Posture]

However, for beginners or people with thick calves, it may be painful. One may feel as if the right and left feet ankles would crack due to overlap. In that case, placing a bag-pillow made of towel, or cotton, between ankles is helpful. Pain gradually disappears with practice, and after a certain period of time, you will be able to stay longer in a stable posture.

Half-lotus posture

There is a slightly easier way for those people who say they cannot meditate because they cannot sit cross-legged in Lotus posture. People with fat calf muscle, or chubby legs may not sit cross-legged comfortably. They may try meditation in half-lotus posture.

Half-lotus posture is when the right ankle is placed on the left knee.

Anyone can do this pose easily, but just when you sit placing your leg on the on one knee, at times you may not keep your balance because it does not stay on the ground. In that case, it is appropriate to place a small padding behind the buttocks. As you sit high, your knees will touch the ground and your back would remain straight.

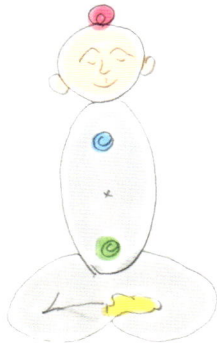

[Half-lotus Posture]

In case of discomfort, place another small padding on top of the sitting pad under the hips. If you sit on it, your buttocks will be raised about 10 Centimeters, thus it would be more comfortable; your legs will be straightened and your posture would be right.

Like pyramid

The tomb of ancient Egyptian kings is called pyramid.

Pyramid was built elaborately. The central point of the pyramid is the place where all the energy gathers, thus even degenerative substances do not rot quickly; this fact is scientifically proved.

The lotus position or the half-lotus position in which the Buddha sits is similar to a pyramid in some ways.

In lotus or half-lotus position, the center is considered as central energy point.

Because belly button area is energy-sea point, if you take the correct posture, the energy in the body would gather at the belly button, or lower abdomen and your entire body would be energy enriched.

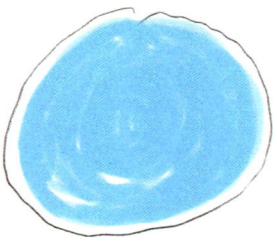

Breathing meditation

Most practitioners at the time of the Buddha practiced breathing meditation to improve self-esteem and focus on the mind. Breathing is part of everyday life, you cannot be separated from it even for a single minute. Breathing is the foundation of life.

Breathing meditation is always inhaling and exhaling, but while inhaling and exhaling, observe your breath constantly. When breathing gets rough, mind also will easily get harsh. When your breathing calms down, the mind also cannot but be calm.

Breathing practice is widely practiced, not only in Buddhism but also in social-space. Although different religions differ in suggesting ways of breathing, the fundamental objective of returning to a clear and quiet mind remains the same, and thus, every one must master breathing.

Method of breathing meditation

Breathing meditation is a meditation that focuses on inhaling and exhaling mindfully. When you breathe in through your nose, air passes through your Lungs and reaches the energy point at lower abdomen and this should be performed with full consciousness. The main concern is awareness when breathing in and breathing out.

As you become accustomed to breathing, your breathing becomes lighter and finer. When breathing comes to a point where you cannot even feel it, then your consciousness deepens and your mind becomes stable.

At first, practice for 10 minutes, then gradually increase to 20 to 30 minutes and then to 1 hour. Rather than practicing for several hours at a time, if you practice consistently and repeatedly, the depth gained from meditation will increase and you will be able to feel the mystery by yourself.

Importance of breathing

Breathing in meditation is as precious as life. Inhalation should not be done with the mouth, but with the nose, and it plays an important role in calming the mind.

Breathing should be calm. When the breathing is rough, the mind gets excited. That is why it is important to calm breathing. The sound of breathing must be light, deep, and quiet enough to be inaudible.

Breathe deep into lower abdominal region and breath out slowly, in sitting position with your hands on your knees.

While breathing in and out, closely observe air passing slowly through the nostrils.

As the breath enters deep through the nostrils to lungs, into the lower abdomen and leaves, be mindful. Continue to count exhaling as 'one' , 'two' and so on. When the count reaches ten, start again from the beginning. If you repeat from ten to ten, your excited mind will gradually calm down and you will gradually feel it. You will feel the sound becoming quieter. As you continue to count the numbers like this, your mind gets absorbed into meditation.

However, when counting goes beyond ten, you become too obsessed with numbers. There are cases where your mind becomes more distracted as it drags along. Therefore, it is better to count to ten, and then count again from one. As you count your breath, the numbers may go wrong sometimes. There are times when you lose track. In that case, just start counting again from the beginning.

As your breathing becomes finer, it will naturally become stable.

If you pay attention not to breathe rough, your body and mind will gradually relax. You will feel more comfortable and lighter.

Observe breathing

You have to watch your breath coming in and out with a very quiet mind. You should feel the touch of air that passes through the nostrils when breath comes in, and similarly feel the breath that goes out. When you breathe deep, your mind too must sense the depth.

In this way, observe the inhalation and exhalation without losing sight of it. As you inhale and exhale, you would feel yourself that your breath becomes deeper, lighter and finer.

During breathing, clear saliva fills your mouth. Saliva starts accumulating in the mouth, meaning that your practice is going well. When the energy in the body

harmonizes, the blocked energy and blood will open and move freely, as clean jade-fountain water collect in the mouth. Just swallow the clean saliva quietly, and it would not be long before your saliva begins to accumulate again. By practicing this repeatedly, body and mind gradually become calm and peaceful.

Just breathe with full attention

There is a saying, 'When you breathe, think only about breathing.' Don't cling to the past, or to the future that hasn't come yet. You must not lose your focus either. Watch your breath while being here and now.

If you practice consistently, your breathing will become calm and light and meditation will gradually get deeper. As you go deeper, your breath becomes more detailed and lighter. If you go one step further and practice breathing more consistently, your breathing will almost feel as if it has ceased, and as if you are not breathing. The deeper your breathe, your mind becomes more stable and calm and you feel happy.

While breathing, do not force yourself to breathe. The act of exerting strength or intentionally holding your breath does not help in meditation.

When you breathe, do not think that you are the person who is breathing. You have to breathe unconsciously without even realizing it.

Importance of the waist

The waist plays the role of a pillar, similar to those in building a house.
If the pillar tilts sideways, the house will soon collapse.
It is important to keep your back straight and perpendicular to the ground.
If your back is straight, the center of your body weight is centered at the bottom, that reduces fatigue and allows you to sit for a long time. Your mind and body feels comfortable.

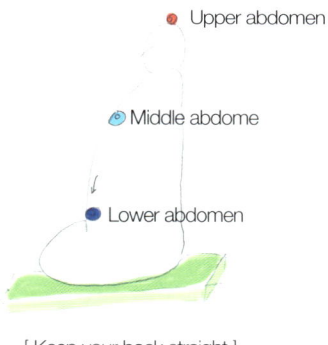

[Keep your back straight]

When you sit with your back straight, the arteries and veins that flow through the body can communicate better and thus, fatigue decreases and mind gets more stable. It helps in the progress. Therefore, posture is more important for beginners than anything else. Also pay attention that your posture is correct even while walking. You have to feel it and watch closely.

[Shape and posture of hands]

Placing of hands?

In a cross-legged or half-lotus position, place the left palm on your right palm, so that the tips of both thumbs lightly touch each other. Thus, an oval-shaped hand structure gets formed between the palm and both thumbs. This oval shape is the Mudra of Dharma realm.

Place both oval-shaped palms gently over the place where your feet intersect. The place where the hands lie is the lower abdomen region.

Placing the open palms on both knees facing the sky is also another way. All you have to do is choose a way to be comfortable and focus on progress.

Then point both palms towards the sky and raise them to chest level. Allow yourself to receive the energy of the universe. At this time, do not put too much strength in both shoulders and make sure that your entire body is relaxed.

Open or close eyes?

The eyes can be slightly open or lightly closed: eyes need not be completely open, just half open is fine.

When you open your eyes wide, objects appear clearly in front of you and you become distracted. When you close your eyes fully, you may feel drowsy. Sit in a relaxed position with your eyes half open and all you have to do is to keep your gaze about 70 or 80 centimeters in front of you.

Shape of mouth and tongue inside?

If you keep your mouth open, your energy will escape. Keep your mouth softly closed. Even if you close your mouth too tightly, it gets in the way to focus.

Place your tongue gently against the roof of your mouth. Place the tip of your tongue against your upper teeth. When the tongue touches the roof of the mouth, the energy in the body and blood circulates well. You will be able to feel that just light touch of tongue to the roof of your mouth stabilizes mind. In everyday life also, you should try to keep the tongue touching the roof of your mouth.

Place of meditation

When meditating, you must first decide on a location; place where you can avoid noise; listening to the sounds of nature would be even better. However, for people living in city, practice meditation in a quiet room, or at a nearby meditation center is more effective. It is better to meditate in a quiet place, where there is no interference from others as much as possible.

Way to practice

Sit cross-legged, straighten your back, and place your hands in Dharma Mudra position on the intersecting feet, eyes half-open. Place your gaze 70 to 80 centimeters ahead and close your mouth lightly.

Please sit in a comfortable position with your tongue against the roof of your mouth. There should not be any pressure on both shoulders. Be reminded that when body is stiff, it easily gets tired.

Check that the height of the seat matches to your body, shake your body to the left and right gently and sit in the most comfortable position. After you have a stable posture, use a technique suitable for you. Then practice observing the inhaling and exhaling of breath and start journey into a world of deep meditation through focused observation.

Master Hyega

Master Hyega inherited the teachings of Master Bodhidharma. Hyega once asked his teacher, "I always feel anxious. Please heal my anxious mind."

"Are you anxious? Then I will comfort your anxious mind. I will teach you my dear, but in order to cure an anxious mind, first find your anxious mind and present it before me. What are you hesitating for? Find it quickly and hand it over to me," he said.

Even though Hyega searches every corner, but could not find his anxious mind.

"Master, I cannot find anxiety anywhere in my mind. When the disciple said this, Master Bodhidharma responded"

"Then the feeling of anxiety was not in your mind from

the beginning. Isn't it so?"

With just one word from the teacher, Hyega gained enlightenment.

Hyega was able to feel at ease in that instant. Sometimes we insist on having something that is not there, and thus, suffer.

We too must realize this fact as Hyega did. The painful and anxious mind did not exist from the beginning.

Hyega was deceived by the shadow of suffering that he had created.

Kinds of Meditation

We get closer to the truth, when we start realizing that there is no hatred, no suffering, no good, no bad in our hearts.

Unobstructed mind

To enter the mind-set of meditation

you must always have a relaxed mind.

Just as a flying bird freely flies across the sky

there should be no hindrance in your mind.

You should feel yourself breathing and be awake.

Pay close attention to each and every movement you make.

If you observe it consistently,

even observation is freed.

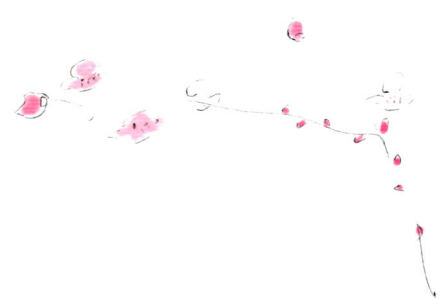

Illusion created by mind

We are suffering endlessly while being guided by the shadows of thoughts arising on the clean foundation of mind.

The mind, like a mirror, reflects things. In short, the fundamental mind is like empty space, like the blue sky, always quiet, clear, clean, and relentless.

Instead of obsessing over all kinds of illusion and desire, and distracting thoughts about seeking salvation, if you shake them all off, your fundamental mind will be clear and clean, and you will be able to see things as they are.

In our hearts, there are inherently no hatred, suffering, good or bad. If you vaguely knew that there was none, you would get closer to the truth.

When observing a mountain, just look at the mountain leisurely, and when seeing water, only the water should be visible.

Seagulls fly leisurely on Haeundae Beach, young people walk shoulder to shoulder on the empty white sandy beach, and in the distance the waves come and go rhythmically.

Just see things as they are without any hesitation.

When a miracle-sound comes, you just hear the sound of miracle, and when someone sings, you just listen to the song. There is no need for any pretense.

If you look at the world with a mind that does not discriminate, the world will remain clear and beautiful.

When the shadow of greed disappears from the mind, the world becomes nothing but beautiful.

Mind without focus

The word means 'without a focus.'

It refers to a clear, untainted mind.

Clear and clean mind,

Still and unmoving,

Like untainted lotus flower

The original mind refers to a peaceful world.

Globalization of meditation

These days, interest in meditation is growing. You can see posters on the street and even western people are drawn to meditation.

There are meditation centers in India and Europe, as well as in Australia and the United States. Among the Asian region, meditation is also practiced in Buddhist meditation centers in Korea.

In particular, Blue-eyed Buddhist monks from foreign countries such as France, United States, Canada, Europe, Southeast Asia etc. are practicing Seon (Korean meditation) and are making good progress. Then why do Westerners want to meditate? Europeans live in relative material abundance. However, they realized the truth that there is a limit to the happiness gained from material posessions.

Capitalism is glamorous, but the gap between the rich and the poor is getting serious. Discrimination against deprived is worsening. Material abundance is gradually becoming a problem for everyone living in this world. Pure beauty is becoming more and more desolate due to material world. Beautiful spiritual world is declining slowly, which is very sad.

Now Westerners also realized how valuable it is to train mind and find happiness from within. That is why they are coming here to get direct experience.

If the first learning goes stray

If you meditate correctly from the start, your mind will become calm.

You will be able to feel it easily. When putting on clothes, if the first button is arranged wrong, it will not look neat, no matter how hard you try.

It is the same with meditation. It helps a lot if one receives meditation training from a good professional teacher.

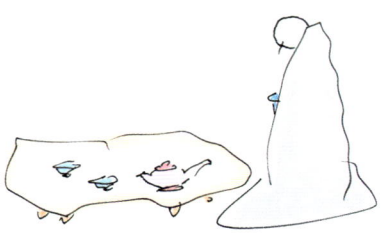

Walking meditation

You can also literally meditate while walking. Walking meditation also relaxes the body and mind. Observe yourself while climbing mountain or strolling on grass. Feel the steps as you walk on the ground. Put hatred, resentment, everything down, and just walk.

When walking on the mountains, observe the trees, grass, and birds chirping.

Walk while listening to the sounds of nature. Just climb the mountain without thinking. When walking, you and the mountain become one. All you have to do is walk quietly, one step at a time, without pretense or show-off.

Just observe trees, rocks, flowers, flowing water, chirping birds and feel it in your mind as you walk. Then the mind gets deeper, wider, and quieter. You will experience this meditation just by yourself.

This space is the transcendent world of pure and beautiful mind.

Lying meditation

Lying meditation is simply lying down as if you were relaxing and contemplating on yourself. It is a meditation on observing self while lying still.

Repeat in your mind six or seven times, 'The right arm is relaxed' and observe. Similarly, repeat that 'the left arm is relaxed' and observe it in your mind.

Observe again while exhaling. Repeat and feel that your right and left arms are relaxing.

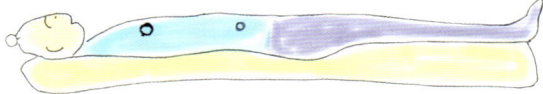

[Lying meditation]

Repeat the same in case of both shoulders, both arms and legs and observe them relaxing. Now do the same considering the whole body and see it getting relaxed, The whole body starts to melt. It is like ice melting in warm air and experience this new consciousness. By such efforts, you can experience samadhi through consistent meditation.

Importance of body relaxation

The important thing in meditation is to relax your body. When your mind is relaxed, your body also relaxes. Relaxing body and mind is essential for meditation.

When you feel tired in your life, your body and mind gets stiff; steady mental observation will gradually help your body relax. It lets you return to your original mind. The home of a peaceful mind is free from quarrels and conflicts.

As your breathing and thoughts become stable, you feel comfortable, and that is paradise: pain and suffering disappear.

When distractions arise

When distracting thoughts arise while meditating, just allow them in. You should try to focus only on breathing and one thought.

If you focus on your breathing like that, distracting thoughts will naturally disappear soon. The mind would quieten incrementally.

Just as muddy water becomes clear when mud sinks to the bottom, your mind becomes peaceful when your mind is clear, and all thoughts that were focused on the outside world come to rest. The mind becomes calm and returns to its original home.

Meditation with music

This kind of meditation is just listening to your favorite music without thinking. If distracting thoughts arise while listening, do not be distracted, just focus on music. As you listen, you surrender your body and mind to the music.

Music makes the heart happy and calms the restless mind. You may listen to music while sitting and, standing, and sometimes while singing.

People who specialize in music believe that as music and song become one, the passion of singing quickly increases the pulse of life.

Even when life is difficult and difficulties come, concentrate on listening to music. Then, music and you can naturally become one.

Tea-drinking meditation

Daseon-il-yeo-seung (禪一如) means 'Tea and seon (zen) are not two things.' Drinking tea is also meditation, and practicing seon is also meditation.

The process of boiling water, adding tea leaves into tea pot, brewing, straining the fragrant tea carefully in a teacup and then drinking it, each and every action here is meditation. Drinking tea without pretense and show-off, is like practicing the path; there is no difference.

Tea has the power to clear the mind. Drinking Dharma tea in the mountains makes the mind clear and calm.

Drinking tea with a mind free of distracting thoughts or wandering thoughts is literally a way to cultivate the path.

Just observation is meditation

Climb the mountain one step at a time.

Sit on a rock, look at silently standing trees, nameless flowers on the way, listen to flowing water in the valley, witness maple leaves fall, enjoy beauty of mountains and valleys, and squirrel's playful run.

Quietly hold breath and watch.

Just observing is meditation.

Just look without pretense or embellishment.

Once your mind gets connected, it is always a leisurely feeling, whether you are in the mountains or in the fields.

Regular meditation

Practice breathing meditation regularly, even for an hour or two a day.

If you observe it, you can feel a change in your personality. Even people who always had an unstable and disorderly mind can feel better when they meditate.

Tense, angry face transform into a gentle look by meditation. Angry outburst on others for small harmless comments change for the better. Angry, over sensitive mind calms down gradually. When your mind becomes quiet, your attitude towards the world relaxes more and more.

While meditating

While meditating

Desire and greed cannot shake me.

While meditating

hatred and resentment disappear.

While meditating

greed and anger also disappear.

After meditating

vain thoughts

is no more able to disturb me.

Effects of meditation

People suffering from high blood pressure,

or impatient ones calm down by meditation.

Blood pressure return to normal.

Meditation relaxes a stiff body. My mind becomes quiet and stable.

Meditation has the power to transform sympathetic nervous system into parasympathetic nervous system.

This is also a medically proven fact.

Original mind

Meditation is about returning to the quiet mind

before any single thought arose in it.

Imagine how was your mind before any thought arose.

Think of your original mind as a white drawing paper before drawing,

Think about the blue sky before the clouds.

The original mind is like the blue sky.

Daily Practice of Meditation

By living each day, every movement and action itself becomes the way and the meditation.

Master Seungchan

Master Seung Chan was suffering from paralysis. Seeing his thin body he realized the impermanence of life and set out on a quest for salvation.

What is a true life? After contemplating on the big task of life and death, he sought help from Master Hyega who was known to possess Taoist power.

"I have a lot of sins in my past life, so I am suffering from this disease. Please have mercy and destroy my sins and save my life."

On hearing the sick man's appeal. Master Hyega said,

"Oh, I see! Please bring to me the sins that you have committed right here. I will destroy them."

Master Seung Chan searched his inner world to find his sins. No matter how hard he searched, he could not find them. Master Seung Chan realized that sin has no self-nature, just a play of the mind, and the mind is inherently

empty.

"Even if you look for sin, there is no way to find it."

"If there is no way to find out your sins, why repent now for all sins that has already gone."

Seungchan gained enlightenment after hearing these words.

"Sinful karma does not have any form. Sin is also inherently as empty as space."

If you remain in a sense of guilt and think that you are a sinner, it will be an endless tunnel of sin. Your thoughts are tied to your body and cause pain and self-suffering.

Have a cup of tea!

Seon Master Jo Ju of China always said, "Have a cup of tea," and served tea to who so ever came to enquire about the path.

No matter who comes, the master said, "Please have a cup of tea." After drinking a cup of tea, some said, "I have learned the path well from you," and left after a big bow. while some others could not understand what he meant and just drank tea and left.

His disciple, who always watched this from the side, was very curious.

 "Whenever someone asks about the path, Master you

always said, 'Have a cup of tea. He asked, 'Is there any deep meaning in those words?

Master Jo Ju, who was listening quietly, had a smile on his face and exclaimed

"Oh, I see. You should also have a cup of tea."

Let me serve a cup of tea to you too, have a cup of tea. The path is contained in these simple words.

Where is the path?

The path is nothing special.

From morning to evening until bedtime

Every single thing in our daily life becomes 'affirmative'

and 'the path'.

It is a teaching about happening of 'Seon'.

While living the day,

Stoping and moving itself

Becomes the path and meditation.

The base of original mind

If you meditate consistently,

you will come to have

mindset without discrimination and

mind without division.

Mind is called 'delicate mind.'

without a cloud,

as a clear and clean sky

Delicate mind is something like the lotus flower

And like the blue sky.

A mind won't shake even when shaken

is the base of original state of mind,

no muddy water can drench

or, pollute it.

It is ever a clear and pure mind.

Mind that resembles home

We all have a home of our mind. The village house where we were born, the school we went to, the back yard of the village, the flowing stream, such familiar images of the old countryside exists in our hearts, even though we live in complex city space.

As our lives confine us to a busy daily life and a set routine, we cannot easily open ourselves to our hometown, even though we remain attached to it.

Meditation is the continued practice that enables us to return to our pure, unspoiled, innocent mind's home that we all aspire for.

Self-satisfaction

The opposite of satisfaction is dissatisfaction.

The cause of all pains can be traced to ignorance about satisfaction.

If you live your life as it is without any attachment,

you will no longer care much about satisfaction or dissatisfaction.

Everything that makes you tired arises from

dissatisfaction, and it could be

called a psychological issue.

Consistent meditation

If you meditate consistently,

mind becomes calm and clear.

Awkward behavior becomes cool.

As you do not live with a restless mind,

you will have a happy life wherever you stop or go.

If your mind is over-anxious, you cannot lead a stable life.

You always need to observe your mind.

When your mind becomes stable and calm,

staying at a place or moving around becomes a matter of joy and happiness.

If you fix it, you will be happy…

It will never be fixed.

I am afraid, I cannot fix it!

Is there anything in this world that cannot be fixed?

Be persistent and try hard.

Don't give up prematurely.

It can definitely be fixed.

You can fix it if you want.

On fixing it you will be calm, and happy.

Look at your self-mind.

Go back to your original calm mind.

On practicing meditation consistently,

Your personality,

and even behavior will eventually change.

A mind like the sky

When you meditate

Mind resembles the blue sky.

There may be rain and wind

Even thunder and lightning

But sky is always blue.

When mind becomes quiet

It resembles the blue sky

That does not change.

Everything is one

The waves arise.

Water droplets splash.

In a calm sea,

when the wind blows, the waves are bound to rise.

Water drops and waves are originally one.

The home of water drops is wave

The home of waves is the water in the sea.

Waves, water-droplets and the sea

are the same.

Water droplets splashing into the sea

Look different, but it is the same sea.

Poor habits

While meditating

Your poor habits change.

Karma exists in everyone.

In self-thoughts

Self-expressions

Your behavior becomes a habit

And create a fixed frame.

A fixed frame is called a stereotype.

Drawn to that frame and self-concept, we live.

If you live tied to a frame,

Life becomes difficult.

Poor thinking makes life difficult.

You can remove the frame of poor ideas through meditation.

If you don't change it to a more relaxed conceptual framework, life becomes increasingly painful.

Meditation and Karma

Due to bad habits

often the entire life is ruined.

Poor old habits

Get difficult to fix.

Words,

Thoughts,

Poor actions

mean 'karma' in Buddhism, .

Karma is acts of

Past life and current life.

Karma is self-created.

Consistent meditation gets rid of poor karma

and develops the strength to change the self.

Avoid anger

The way to correct poor karma is
consistent effort.
Anger over small things becomes karma.
Anger, not only causes self-suffering,
but suffering to others around.
Even domesticated dogs hide their tail
in distress when their master is angry.
There is a difference between
angry and the not angry.
When you get angry, happiness dries away.
Conversely, happiness comes
to those who live with a smile.
Controlling anger is meditation.

When angry

When angry

look in the mirror

An angry face cannot be beautiful.

Flushed red eyes,

flushed cheeks,

frozen expressions,

cause great discomfort

to self and others.

Learn to control your anger

Watch yourself consistently

Mistakes will be taken care naturally

on self-correction…

When the anger disappears,

not just the self,

but everyone around become happier.

Meditation in everyday life

Meditation doesn't necessarily have to be done while sitting.

The practice of Seon(Zen) while walking is called Haengseon (行禪).

Practicing lying down is called Waseon.

When you meditate in quiet silence, while sitting, standing, going and coming,

mind becomes clear and calm and is not agitated easily, over any small or big thing.

You will gain the unwavering power of meditation.

Thoughts change to a healthy level, as the mind is not attracted by matter and shape. Karma would resolve, as mind naturally clears.

Donkey's grave

A young villager in Tibet set off on a pilgrimage on a donkey that was raised by him with great love and care.

The pilgrimage trail was long and difficult, and it was certainly more difficult for a donkey to move around with the rider.

The weather was very hot that day.

The donkey was very tired.

"Master, can we rest a bit and get some water?" the donkey suggested.

The owner decided to take a little rest.

Fortunately, there was shade of a tree and a shabby

empty farmhouse nearby, so they decided to rest there.

The owner fetched water from a nearby well and served it to the donkey who had given him good ride.

On a difficult pilgrimage, a donkey is like a precious treasure.

When the pilgrim woke up, the sky was full of glittering stars and the moon was still floating.

The young man thought it would be much easier if he started the journey a bit early on a cool night like this.

He tried to awake the donkey sleeping next to him by a little push.

But the donkey did not wake up, as he had already left this world.

He was deeply sorry for the donkey that had left for the other world without even a good meal.

Young pilgrims could have abandoned the dead donkey and move on the pilgrimage trail but he did not.

There was no one around, so he had to bury the donkey all by himself. He dug up earth all night and covered the donkey's body. As the donkey was large, the tomb had to be large as well.

After burying the donkey, he was so tired that he fell asleep beside the tomb. He didn't know how long he had slept, but suddenly he heard some noise around.

He slept as he was very tired. On waking up and looking around, he found that many people had gathered. Flowers, fruits, and rice cakes were placed on the donkey's tomb. They had also raised money and each person made their bowing-wish. One of them came up and asked the young pilgrim, "who is the great saint buried here?"

Looking at the size of the tomb, there is no doubt that a great saint must be enshrined there. Who is the great saint in this tomb?

The pilgrim could not answer that a donkey was buried here. Many believers had gathered and had bowed to the tomb. If he said it was the tomb of a donkey, many people would be very disappointed. He answered that the person buried here was a great saint, who had sweated carrying burden of others all his life, but never spoke a word.

One by one, the people worshiped the tomb and deified the saint who has no name but carried the burdens for others. The number of such visits to the tomb gradually kept increasing.

The young pilgrim had no choice but to become the owner of the donkey's shrine that was worshiped, and supported his livelihood with the offerings made by the people.

There are people who by following the path taken by others without prior knowledge and reach a destination never seen or heard before. People talk about the paradise in the world of knowledge.

The pilgrim was amazed by the noise of the people and was just lead away by it. Most of the people follow or are led away like this. It is like people knowing nothing and bowing to the donkey's grave.

Well, nothing could be any better!

A pilgrim on the path of truth often follows the one he wants to take.

You have to figure out how to get there on your own.

There are groups of people everywhere who deceive people by imitating saints.

Thus, you must also look back and reflect on yourself.

You need to check yourself if the path you are taking is the right path.

The path to truth exists within one's inner world.

It is not good enough to tell the truth this way, or other way.

If you take a pilgrimage along the path of meditation, you will find out by yourself which place is the paradise.

It is something that you can realize and know for yourself.

Meditation makes your mind happy on its own.

We all must walk the path of meditation and feel happiness along the way.

The Strength of Meditation

The power of concentration has the power to change life. Change of personality through meditation makes life beautiful and happy.

Why am I here now?

In this wide space

Among the endless stars

Why am I here?

I don't even know where I arrived and

I don't even know where to go.

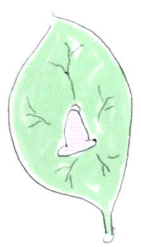

Meditation and Samadhi

The mind is like water. In clear and calm water you can see the fish at play. But when the wind blows, ripples appear on the water and the water turns muddy, then you have no idea what is in the water. You cannot even see through it.

If you meditate, you can achieve samadhi. Smadhi is a state of tranquility that puts an end to the noisy and delusive thoughts. The mind becomes still, without wandering.

Practicing meditation means constantly controlling wavering thoughts to keep it from continued wandering.

When you sit on meditation, you may see that your wandering thoughts arise like boiling porridge. This is like opening the window in an unused room to allow wind to drive out the dust that had piled up, but in the process, the dust rises even more.

However, if you wipe the room regularly, dust does not rise. Similarly, on continued practice of meditation, mind becomes increasingly clear and calm.

A soft mind

When I look at the autumn sky

so clear and clean that it hurts eyes

and it seems like kissing the sky

face to face.

This mind is like the autumn sky

Clear and clean.

That clear mind

because of the stains of desire and greed

gets spotty and dirty.

Take a close look

The heart is a place where dirt cannot stay,

when examined closely.

Just as there is no stain on the sky,

dirt cannot remain buried in the mind either.

As the sky has no shape

mind is also formless.

If you empty your mind from thoughts

it resembles the sky

always tender.

Power of concentration

Meditation helps you to get rid of distractions and increase concentration of mind. If you work without focus, your work efficiency will not increase. That is why meditation must be practiced consistently in daily life.

Whether you are moving or stopping, sitting, or standing, you must practice meditation as daily routine and be one with it in life. Students with improved concentration are bound to see their grades improving. The power to focus is the power to change life. The change of personal qualities through meditation makes life beautiful and happy.

Calming excited mind

Wavering and scattered thoughts are like a monkey tied to a post. Our thoughts do not remain still even for a moment, and keep moving constantly from one thought to another. A distracted and un-calm mind is thus, compared to a monkey.

Even though one is alone in the room, his thoughts are noisy like a market place. One is always thinking about time gone by and worrying what could happen in future ahead. In this sense, meditation is a practice that transforms complex thoughts into a calm mind.

Meditation has the power to change a monkey-like excited mind into a calm mind.

Like pebbles

Go out to the beach.

The sea is churning.

The sea water is alive and dancing.

The beach is covered with countless sand and pebbles.

Each stone has a different color and size.

Each appearance is also different.

Every pebble has its own personality;

Big stones, small stones, angular stones.

A pebble doesn't cry because it's ugly.

Every appearance has a charm.

Even when the sea waves push, it will neither lament, nor suffer any pain.

'Cause I'm a pebble

No matter where and when life takes shape

Just accept it and live with it.

Just live like the pebbles on the beach.

Source of thoughts

Where there is water, you just see the water. Where there are flowers, you just see the beauty of flowers. Just watch and listen to the chirping birds without any pretense or prior thinking.

It is the mind that sees, hears, and knows all things clearly. This present space is honest, without pretense, and remains calm. This place is the true seat of the original mind.

This original mind is so calm that all images remain uncut and even last forever. It is so clear and clean, that no image is dark. Therefore, the original mind is the source of my thoughts.

Transform your Karma

When karma transforms, over-excited mind calms down.

Mind becomes deep like a sea.

Restlessness disappears and mind becomes calm.

Gradually, this mind changes to that of a saint.

Shadow created by thoughts

Enlightenment has the power to distinguish between truth and lies.

How many people laugh and cry, driven by desire and greed?

Most people go down the path of desire and greed. They mistakenly believe that this is the ultimate happiness. Desire and greed are like a haze. It appears, and soon disappears. It appears and disappears again and again.

Everyone paints a picture with their thoughts in their mind. That picture is just an illusion. It makes us sad, it pains us. Everything that makes me sad and gives me a hard time was created by my thoughts and when you know at the instant that it was a ruined shadow, you will be deceived by it no more.

I am a happy man

Just quietly look at yourself.

Just look at yourself, being detached!

You are a happy person.

You have infinite possibilities.

Your inner world is full of joy and happiness.

Feel satisfaction and gratitude even for small things.

The fact that I am here is happiness and joy.

Just watch and listen

When spring comes

Flowers bloom

Freshness of sprouting buds

Chirping of birds

Sound of a flowing stream

See with your eyes

Listen with your ears

Just see

Just listen.

A free man

As you live your life, you become tied to money and fame without even realizing it. We end up living tied down by various desires and greed: Tied to family network, tied to work, tied to everything around. This is why we live a difficult life. However, if you look closely, money, fame, did not tie you up, you tied to them yourself.

No one can tie me down. I myself created a framework called obsession and got entangled into it. When you break through the framework of possessiveness and obsession, you will finally be able to become a free man.

Epilogue

So far, you have been on a meditation journey with me.

How was it?

There must have been a time when winds, waves, and people accompanying you were of no hindrance to you.

Now look into your 'daily self,' putting all aside, with humility and calm mind.

You will surely find yourself much more comfortable and stable.

Now,

I am facing the happy you.

I am with the fragrant you.

I hope that this journey offered to you will be a beautiful gift that will protect 'us' for a long time.

Translated by. Alok Kumar Roy
Professor Emeritus, Busan University of Foreign Studies, Busan, South Korea
Director, International Relations, Association of Korean Buddhist Culture (AKBC)
Advisor, English Research Center of Buddhist Texts (ERCEBT)

Meditation Journey of Bikkhu Jeong Yeo
A Meditation Journey for Seeking Myself

Written and illustrated by Seon. Master Jeongyeo

First edition, 1st printing. June 15, 2025

Published by. Kim Yun-hee
Designed by. Bang Hye-young
Publisher. puremind Books
Publication Registration. July 10, 2000 No. 02-01-295
Address. 14-3, 125 Jwasuyeong-ro, Suyeong-gu, Busan (2nd floor)
Tel. 051) 255-0263
Fax. 051) 255-0953
E-mail. puremind-ms@daum.net

ⓒ Master Jeongyeo 2014. The copyright of this book belongs to the author. It is prohibited to quote or interfere with any or part of the contents without the permission of the author and the publisher.

Not for sale
ISBN 978-89-94782-25-6 03200